C000020195

STATIONS
of the **Cross**
then and now

By the same author

The Gospel of Luke
The Gospel of Mark
Emmaus: the gracious visit of God
Jesus and the Gospels
Where Does the Jesus Story Begin?
Impressions of Jesus
The Parables of Jesus
Praying with Pictures
Waiting on God (also e-book)
Journeying with Jesus: a companion's guide
Journeying with Jesus: a guide for groups
Journeying towards Jesus in Advent
Borrowing the Eyes of Others: paintings vol. 1
Awakening to Yourself: paintings vol. 2
Seasons of the Word: reflections on the Sunday readings
Diary for the Year of Faith
Diary for the Year of Matthew
Diary for the Year of Mark
Praying the Rosary: a journey through scripture and art (also e-book)
Diary for the Year of Mercy
Journeying with Jonah: the struggle to find yourself

Electronic

Jesus and the Gospels: 36 lectures on CD
Reflecting on Paintings: 10 reflections on CD
Where Does the Jesus Story Begin?: 10 lectures on CD
Seasons of the Word: Complete reflections on CD
Journeying with Jonah: 2 lectures on CD

The Gospel of John (DVD)
The Power of the Parables (DVD)
The Passion Narratives in the Gospels (DVD)
The Transfiguration in the Gospels and in Life (DVD)
The Discipleship Journey (DVD): with David Wells

STATIONS
of the **Cross**
then and now

Denis McBride C.Ss.R.

Published by Redemptorist Publications
Alphonsus House, Chawton, Hampshire, GU34 3HQ, UK
Tel. +44 (0)1420 88222, Fax. +44 (0)1420 88805
Email rp@rpbooks.co.uk, www.rpbooks.co.uk

A registered charity limited by guarantee
Registered in England 3261721

Copyright © Denis McBride 2016
First published December 2016

Edited by Peter Edwards
Designed by Eliana Thompson

ISBN 978-0-85231-472-2

All rights reserved. No part of this publication may be reproduced, stored in a retrieval system, or transmitted in any form or by any means, electronic, mechanical, photocopying, recording or otherwise, without prior permission in writing from Redemptorist Publications.

The moral right of the author to be identified as the author of this work has been asserted in accordance with the Copyright, Designs and Patents Act 1988.

A CIP catalogue record for this book is available from the British Library.

The publisher gratefully acknowledges permission to use the following copyright material:

Excerpts from the New Revised Standard Version of the Bible: Anglicised Edition, © 1989. 1995, Division of Christian Education of the National Council of the Churches of Christ in the United States of America. Used by permission. All rights reserved.

Psalms from the Grail Psalter reprinted by permission of HarperCollins Publishers Ltd © 1963.

Printed by Lithgo Press Ltd.,
Leicester, LE8 6NU

For
Mary and Danny Ferry
wife and husband
sister and brother-in-law
beloved friends

Contents

Introduction

Around the nave of nearly every Catholic church in the world, you can see a series of simple crosses or fourteen images depicting the passion of Jesus, moving from his condemnation by Pontius Pilate to his burial in a borrowed tomb: they are known as the Stations of the Cross. The original devotion began in Jerusalem where pilgrims would follow in the footsteps of Jesus, usually beginning at the palace of Herod, where Jesus was condemned, and finishing at the traditional site of Jesus' tomb.

By the fifth century, there was a growing interest in the Church to replicate the holy places at home so that people unable to travel to the Holy Land could make a pilgrimage in heart and mind. For example, St Petronius, Bishop of Bologna, who died around AD 450, constructed a series of chapels at the monastery of San Stefano, memorialising key moments in Jesus' passion journey.

William Wey, an English priest and pilgrim, visited the Holy Land in 1462 and is credited with the first use of the term "stations" – referring to halting-places in Jerusalem in memory of Jesus' passion (see *The Itineraries of William Wey*, edited and translated into modern English by Francis Davey, published by the Bodleian Library, Oxford). Wey's vivid narrative describes the manner in which a pilgrim followed the steps of Jesus through fourteen stations, although only five of them correspond to our traditional list. In different countries the number of stations varied between seven and thirty; it was not until 1731 that Pope Clement XII fixed the number of stations at fourteen.

The longest chronicle about Jesus in all four Gospels is the passion narrative. Each Gospel develops the drama through five acts:

1. Jesus in Gethsemane
2. Jesus before the Jewish authority
3. Jesus before the Roman authority
4. Jesus' crucifixion and death
5. Jesus' burial in the tomb.

One striking feature of all four accounts is how spare and reserved the evangelists are in describing the brutality that Jesus endured: none of them dwells on Jesus' excruciating suffering either on the way of the cross or on the cross itself.

I have chosen Curd Lessig's *Way of the Cross* to accompany my reflections and prayers: for me, these stations have a graceful spareness about them. (The original set can be seen in Holy Trinity Church, in the Bavarian village of Gemünden am Main, in the diocese of Würzburg.) Lessig is a craftsman and church painter whose murals, stained glass and paintings adorn churches and public buildings throughout southern Germany. His work is characterised by a deep faith and a solemn simplicity. Like the evangelists, he does not dwell on the physical suffering of Jesus during the passion: his Jesus proceeds with majesty and purpose and composure along the road of suffering to keep his appointment with death.

The format of each of the following stations is simple:

    a. A passage from scripture
    b. Curd Lessig's painting
    c. Reflection on the scripture passage and the particular station
    d. A modern photograph
    e. Meditation on the chosen image
    f. Final prayer.

I have called the book *Stations of the Cross – then and now* in an attempt to recognise that the way of the cross winds through every village, town and city in our world. The way of sorrows was not only an ancient road located in Jerusalem two thousand years ago; it is a crowded highway, populated by millions of people who endure violence and suffering today. These fourteen Stations of the Cross serve not only to celebrate the memory of Jesus' passion but also as a way to become more alert to the passion of so many around us who struggle under the burden of their own cross.

I did not write these stations for public performance but for personal devotion: anyone can make the way of the cross at home. After all, it is there, for many people, that they live out their own suffering. Reflecting on one station might prove sufficient for the day. For the special time of Holy Week, however, given that there are fourteen stations, reading one in the morning and one in the evening would take you up to Holy Saturday and the tomb.

These reflections can also be used as a course book for Lent, for people coming together to reflect not only on the passion of Jesus but on how that way of sorrows persists today. How would you link that time-honoured story to the suffering in our world today? What modern images would you select to put beside the ancient Stations of the Cross?

The way of the cross is so familiar to us that we are no longer shocked by the brutality the story contains. In psychology, desensitisation is defined as the diminished emotional response to a negative stimulus after repeated exposure to it. A few of the modern images I have chosen, however, may shock you: I have not chosen them to upset anyone but to arouse awareness of how the passion story in all its savagery continues in our own time. Jesus speaks to us about this in the parable of the last judgement, when he locates his real presence amidst those who suffer in the midst of an ordinary day. The Gospel comes alive best when the story of Jesus and our own story meet and merge: we learn not only that the story of Jesus throws light on our own but, paradoxically, that our own story can throw new light on the story of Jesus.

With deep gratitude I would like to acknowledge our creative designer Eliana Thompson for her inspired work in creating the look and feel of the book; also Ellen McBride, Nicole Barber and Sylvia Perrins for reading the manuscript and making helpful comments.

THE FIRST STATION

Jesus is condemned to death

Scripture

As soon as it was morning, the chief priests held a consultation with the elders and scribes and the whole council. They bound Jesus, led him away, and handed him over to Pilate. Pilate asked him, "Are you the King of the Jews?" He answered him, "You say so." Then the chief priests accused him of many things. Pilate asked him again, "Have you no answer? See how many charges they bring against you." But Jesus made no further reply, so that Pilate was amazed.

Now at the festival he used to release a prisoner for them, anyone for whom they asked. Now a man called Barabbas was in prison with the rebels who had committed murder during the insurrection. So the crowd came and began to ask Pilate to do for them according to his custom. Then he answered them, "Do you want me to release for you the King of the Jews?" For he realised that it was out of jealousy that the chief priests had handed him over. But the chief priests stirred up the crowd to have him release Barabbas for them instead. Pilate spoke to them again, "Then what do you wish me to do with the man you call the King of the Jews?" They shouted back, "Crucify him!" Pilate asked them, "Why, what evil has he done?" But they shouted all the more, "Crucify him!" So Pilate, wishing to satisfy the crowd, released Barabbas for them; and after flogging Jesus, he handed him over to be crucified.

Mark 15:1-15

Reflection

When you heard the litany of charges made against you, dear Lord, why did you not protest your innocence, scream in dissent? Why remain stubbornly silent, so that even the Roman governor stood beside you, amazed at your submission? You knew this was coming, for sure, so why did you not hire a decent defence lawyer? Why were there witnesses only for the prosecution? Where were your chosen followers and the multitude of people you had tended and liberated? For all that passionate outreach of yours, you end up standing alone.

Why did you not confront the assembled vacuum of authority in front of you? In your trial I am told that the chief priests and scribes stirred up the people against you; yet you who had stirred the hearts of so many and spoke with such authority, unlike those same scribes, now remain a silent onlooker of your own fate. Did you even flinch or sigh when you heard the verdict? Was this your curious courtesy of enduring what was handed to you, whatever you settled for? Why, tell me, Lord, were you so serene and accepting? As Seamus Heaney noted:

> When soldiers mocked
> Blindfolded Jesus and he didn't strike back
>
> They were neither shamed nor edified, although
> Something was made manifest – the power
> Of power not exercised, of hope inferred
>
> By the powerless forever.[1]

Is that right? Did you really settle for this? Or is this the result of all you had done throughout your travels in Galilee and Judaea? Given the people you chose to stand beside, the malcontents you attended, the travelling emergency ward that followed you for support, the religious authorities you cartooned and dismissed, is it really any wonder? I mean, really? Don't tell me you were surprised, dear Lord; I would honestly guess not.

You are a northerner, a countryman, at home in the hills of Galilee, in the forgettable hill village of Nazareth. Why not stay like your village – forgettable – and survive? Why is your survival so unimportant to you?

After your time with that wilderness prophet, John the Baptist, you had to leave your home place and make your mark on a wider world. Your mentor, the Baptist, was executed by a vacillating authority in Herod Antipas who feared the disapproval of others; when you heard news of this you wisely retired to a lonely place. Perhaps you should have stayed there. In that place and at that time, did it not cross your mind that you might end up following John in a similar fate? Now you are to be executed by a dithering governor afraid of the disapproval of others. How history repeats itself.

You headed south to Jerusalem as though this destination was compass-fixed in your head. The northerner heads south; the highlander aims for the big city; the Galilean journeys to Judaea. Sometimes we end up in the wrong place, far from the ease of our home place. But, it has to be said in your favour, you were never nostalgic about Nazareth.

I think your most intelligent disciple, Thomas, read you well when he countered the other disciples' advice to avoid heading south by protesting: "Let us also go, that we may die with him." It has to be said there was no spontaneous chorus of agreement. Thomas knew you were fixed on Jerusalem and would not be forestalled. He also knew the inevitable outcome of the destination, unlike the others, and volunteered to share the same fate. Neither he, unsurprisingly, nor the others turned up to join you.

The indecisive Pontius Pilate hoped that offering the criminal Barabbas as an alternative for release to the crowds would surely secure yours. But the crowds howled not for your release but for your execution. You did not demur, of course, as if this were simply a village contest about popularity. Now you move from the active voice, where you made things happen, to the passive voice, where you are handed over to wait on the decision of others. So the passion begins.

Via Dolorosa

Red chairs turn Marshal Tito Street in Sarajevo into a modern Via Dolorosa – a way of sorrows – which continued for more than half a mile. In April 2012, twenty years after the beginning of the siege of Sarajevo, 825 lines of empty chairs were laid out in this main street, representing the 11,541 victims who were condemned to death during the siege.

This was a silent assembled protest against brutality. Some chairs were smaller than the others, to represent the children – more than 1,500 of them – killed by sniper fire and mortar from Bosnian Serb positions on the hills surrounding the city. On these chairs, people placed flowers, teddy bears and toys.

The Bosnian Serbs laid siege to the city of Sarajevo in early April 1992. Their principal target was the Muslim population but they killed many other Bosnian Serbs as well as Croats with attacks that went on for forty-four months, considered the longest siege in modern history.

A concert by the famous Bosnian cellist Vedran Smajlovic also took place. He played his cello in the streets of the besieged city during the war and, along with some of his musical colleagues, risked his life to express his protest and demonstrate his spirit of resistance.

During the war, a number of journalists – both local and foreign – grew frustrated by the denial of the international community, which for years ignored the sufferings of blameless people in Bosnia and refused to be engaged in bringing that suffering to an end. But those 11,541 red chairs, which glistened in the sun in central Sarajevo, are a stunning reminder that we must always stand beside the innocents who are condemned to death.

Prayer

Wilt thou forgive that sin where I begun,
      Which was my sin, though it were done before?
Wilt thou forgive that sin, through which I run,
      And do run still, though still I do deplore?
           When thou hast done, thou hast not done,
           For I have more.

Wilt thou forgive that sin which I have won
      Others to sin, and made my sin their door?
Wilt thou forgive that sin which I did shun
      A year or two, but wallow'd in, a score?
           When thou hast done, thou hast not done,
           For I have more.

I have a sin of fear, that when I have spun
      My last thread, I shall perish on the shore;
But swear by thyself, that at my death thy Son
      Shall shine as he shines now, and heretofore;
           And, having done that, thou hast done;
           I fear no more.

John Donne,
"A Hymn to God the Father"

THE SECOND STATION

Jesus accepts the cross

Scripture

Then he began to teach them that the Son of Man must undergo great suffering, and be rejected by the elders, the chief priests, and the scribes, and be killed, and after three days rise again. He said all this quite openly. And Peter took him aside and began to rebuke him. But turning and looking at his disciples, he rebuked Peter and said, "Get behind me, Satan! For you are setting your mind not on divine things but on human things."

He called the crowd with his disciples, and said to them, "If any want to become my followers, let them deny themselves and take up their cross and follow me. For those who want to save their life will lose it, and those who lose their life for my sake, and for the sake of the gospel, will save it. For what will it profit them to gain the whole world and forfeit their life?"

Mark 8:31-36

Reflection

You accepted the cross, dear Lord, long before it was laid on your shoulders, didn't you? To you it came not as surprise but as destiny. You sensed that this instrument of torture would somehow not only test you but define you. Not long into your ministry you seemed sure that you would have to pay a price for who you are, the awkward people you loved in your spendthrift way, the authorities you castigated and the values you cherished. And the price would be high – yourself.

At the beginning of your ministry it looked possible that the authorities would violently dismiss you; then as your mission developed it looked highly likely; now, of course, it is inevitable. You knew you would have to suffer for the choices you made and you shared that quite openly with your disciples: that your kind of love would make its way with a cross on its back.

I must say I sympathise with Simon Peter when he took you aside that day in Caesarea Philippi to admonish you for all this distressing talk of suffering. To me he sounds like a reasonable road manager giving advice to the principal performer, worrying that people would be confused if that particular speech were ever to be repeated. He must have thought: it is hardly an enticement to follow the master when he reveals that his destination is the killing fields outside Jerusalem. Who is going to leave the security of home and family to follow your forecast of sure turbulence ahead?

And, of course, events would prove Peter right on that score: none of them did follow you to the killing fields, did they?

I admire you for many things, dear Lord, but this especially: what people rarely mention in ordinary conversation is the cost of things – not materially, I mean, but the physical and mental and spiritual heartache and grief that can follow from the choices we all make as we struggle to find a purpose and direction in our lives. You decided to bring to the fore in conversation what most people choose to hide: that suffering is part of everyday life and every relationship, and if people never mention it, they are kidding you.

You have, if I may say so, this annoying habit of attending to what we all want to wish away. For you, suffering is part of everyone's agenda, which is why you challenged all of us to take up our own cross and follow you.

Did you know, dear Lord, that you would bear not only a wooden cross on your shoulders but a world of fatigue and misery and iniquity on your back? You took it all on personally as you criticised your opponents for doing the opposite:

> They tie up heavy burdens, hard to bear, and lay them on the shoulders of others; but they themselves are unwilling to lift a finger to move them.

You know that some authorities have a compulsion to diminish their subjects; they are experts in restricting people's modest freedom to move with dignity and purpose, by imposing needless burdens on them. Not all, but some authorities are sadistic by nature, taking delight in how their fitful demands are unreachable, except by a few perfectionists. And then, when these authorities are approached with pleas for mercy, they turn away and shrug, as if failure and vulnerability are foreign to their very nature. As the Irish poet Patrick Kavanagh observed:

> Their hands push closed the doors that God holds open.[2]

By comparison you proclaimed one of the most beautiful messages I have ever heard:

> Come to me, all you that are weary and are carrying heavy burdens, and I will give you rest. Take my yoke upon you, and learn from me; for I am gentle and humble in heart, and you will find rest for your souls. For my yoke is easy, and my burden is light.

Beloved Lord, what have we done to your yoke, the one you assured us was easy to shoulder? What have we done to your burden, the one you assured us was light?

Accepting the cross

El Salvador is a small Catholic country in Central America named after Christ the Saviour. Between 1979 and 1992 a violent civil war was fought: more than 75,000 people were killed; another 8,000 went missing; nearly a million people were made homeless. All these people were brutally dismissed to the passive voice: they were not consulted about their fate as powerful others made decisions about them.

Monsignor Oscar Romero was made Archbishop of San Salvador in 1977, an appointment that was welcomed by the military regime because Romero was seen to be reliably conservative. Later that year, however, the new archbishop had a conversion experience when he prayed beside the body of his murdered priest friend Rutilio Grande, a heroic spokesman for the rights of poor people. Romero began to look at his country through the eyes of the victims. He realised that if he were to follow in the footsteps of Father Grande, it would, as he wrote, "put me on the road to Calvary". He accepted his cross, acknowledging that the price would be himself.

He became "the voice of the voiceless". Nearly every Sunday, from the pulpit of his cathedral, he denounced the previous week's atrocities – naming who had been killed, who was being tortured and who had disappeared. When advised to have a bodyguard, Romero replied: "Why should the shepherd have protection when his sheep are still prey to wolves?" On the Sunday before his assassination, he addressed the military directly in his radio broadcast, commanding them as their archbishop to stop killing innocent people.

The following day, 24 March 1980, a lone assassin was driven to the hospital chapel where Romero was celebrating Mass. The professional killer used the car door as his rifle rest: he needed only one shot. Before the archbishop fell backwards, the blood from his shattered heart mixed with the hosts on the altar. In that moment time buckled: two passion stories merged into one.

Prayer

The Lord is my light and my help;
whom shall I fear?
The Lord is the stronghold of my life;
before whom shall I shrink?

Though an army encamp against me
my heart would not fear.
Though war break out against me
even then would I trust.

There is one thing I ask of the Lord,
for this I long,
to live in the house of the Lord,
all the days of my life,
to savour the sweetness of the Lord,
to behold his temple.

And now my head shall be raised
above my foes who surround me
and I shall offer within his tent
a sacrifice of joy.

Instruct me, Lord, in your way;
on an even path lead me.
False witnesses rise against me,
breathing out fury.

I am sure I shall see the Lord's goodness
in the land of the living.
Hope in him, hold firm and take heart.
Hope in the Lord!

From Psalm 27

THE THIRD STATION

Jesus falls
the first time

Scripture

Who has believed what we have heard?
And to whom has the arm of the Lord been revealed?
For he grew up before him like a young plant,
and like a root out of dry ground;
he had no form or majesty that we should look at him,
nothing in his appearance that we should desire him.
He was despised and rejected by others;
a man of suffering and acquainted with infirmity;
and as one from whom others hide their faces
he was despised, and we held him of no account.

Surely he has borne our infirmities
and carried our diseases;
yet we accounted him stricken,
struck down by God, and afflicted.
But he was wounded for our transgressions,
crushed for our iniquities;
upon him was the punishment that made us whole,
and by his bruises we are healed.

Isaiah 53:1-5

Reflection

Was it the weight of the cross, dear Lord, or the thought of where this road would take you that made you fall? Often it's what lies ahead of us that wearies us, not the burdens we are carrying now. The danger that lies in store can distract us – that unfinished stretch of road that awaits our footfall. Whatever far horizons you might have contemplated back in the shelter of the hills of Galilee, now real life interrupts and rudely shortens the perspective. You know this is your final journey and it will take you, step by step, to one place and one ending.

When you keeled over, did you ever wonder why all that compassion you shared throughout your shortened ministry had led you to this moment: the costly kindnesses, the risky associations? Why is gentleness so often rudely rewarded, as if it were frailty of mind rather than strength of spirit?

When you smashed into the ground, did you regret anything more than your painful landing? You know how it is when things go wrong: your life suddenly goes in reverse and so much becomes self-evident from the painful place you now inhabit; everything is on display, everyone knows, and now you have faultless visibility. The review, however, is as crushing as it is clear.

Lying on the ground, dazed, were you perhaps troubled for a moment by imaginings? That you could have settled for a peaceful life in Galilee, far from this dangerous city, rented a wee cottage by the Sea of Galilee and asked Simon Peter to teach you how to fish? After all, you did prove you had an instinct for where the fish gathered when you directed Simon to go out into the deep and stop hugging familiar shores. You had an intuition about deep waters, a suspicion of the shallows. After that impressive haul your disciples netted from the sea, dear Lord, you could have been the fishing overseer in Capernaum with a genius for destination.

But I guess this was never an option.

Did you ever think of a peaceful life, far away from threat and trouble? Ever dream of settling down, marrying a loving woman and raising a family in that hideout of Nazareth? Teaching your kids the glories of the tradition you were raised in and the wonders of working with your hands? Forget fishing, then, was carpentry ever a trade to settle into, like it was for Joseph? Being an artisan would have meant you could have travelled with your craft around the country, rather than being tied down to living by the lake as a fisherman. A harmless occupation, it has to be said, and not one likely to disturb the edgy authorities. Who, tell me, would be threatened by a woodworker from the hills?

But I guess this was never an option.

Where you are now, dear Jesus, was ever your only option. So here you are on the rough ground, your face slammed into dirt. No one tends you; no one speaks to you; no one lifts you up. A cast of pitiless onlookers watches and waits for you to get back on your feet. No one wants you to die on the way: they would be deprived of the planned final scene of this brutal street theatre. That would be unfair, after all.

You pick yourself up, take up the cross and place it on your shoulders, steady yourself, adjusting the weight to find the least painful resting place, but all you do is shift the load from bruise to bruise. The earlier flogging, carried out by specialists in brutality, has ensured there is no unbruised spot on your upper body. You take a few steps before you find your faltering rhythm again. You can hear a sigh of relief as the procession starts off again.

While your bruises hurt afresh, dear Lord, I know, again and again, that it is by your wounds that we are healed.

A pope falls

The world was his stage and he strode across it with immense confidence, greeting and meeting and addressing millions of people. The first non-Italian pope in 455 years, Cardinal Karol Wojtyla of Poland was elected in 1978, choosing the name John Paul II. He became the most widely travelled pontiff in the history of the papacy, but Vatican officials were seriously worried about his safety during his frequent contacts with enthusiastic crowds wherever he travelled.

Three years after his election, on 13 May 1981 in St Peter's Square at Vatican City, Pope John Paul II was shot and wounded by Mehmet Ali Ağca. All four bullets, fired from about fifteen feet away, hit John Paul II: two of them lodged in his lower intestine while the other two hit his left index finger and right arm.

Falling back into the popemobile, he was helped by aides and bodyguards as he was driven into the Vatican complex and from there by ambulance to hospital. He suffered severe blood loss and surgeons operated on him for five hours, eventually leading to recovery. It was not long before the travels began again.

Ağca was apprehended immediately, and later sentenced to life in prison by an Italian court. The Pope later forgave his assailant for the assassination attempt. He was pardoned by the Italian president at the Pope's request and was deported to Turkey in June 2000.

This photograph catches a distinct moment: you see authority become helpless, now depending on the support of others; you see vigour become vulnerability, now unable to manage on its own resources.

You see the passion story anew: moral leadership and powerlessness. This was a station in John Paul's Via Dolorosa that would end with his prolonged illness, a time where he believed he was sharing in the passion of the Lord. All the time St John Paul walked his way of the cross, he walked it in the shadow of his Lord.

Prayer

Have mercy on me, God, men crush me;
they fight me all day long and oppress me.
My foes crush me all day long,
for many fight proudly against me.

When I fear, I will trust in you,
in God, whose word I praise.
In God I trust, I shall not fear;
what can mortal man do to me?

All day long they distort my words,
all their thought is to harm me.
They band together in ambush,
track me down and seek my life.

You have kept an account of my wanderings;
you have kept a record of my tears;
(are they not written in your book?)
Then my foes will be put to flight
on the day that I call to you.

This I know, that God is on my side.
In God, whose word I praise,
(in the Lord whose word I praise,)
in God I trust; I shall not fear;
what can mortal man do to me?

From Psalm 56

THE FOURTH STATION

Jesus meets his mother

Scripture

Then Jesus told them a parable about their need to pray always and not to lose heart. He said, "In a certain city there was a judge who neither feared God nor had respect for people. In that city there was a widow who kept coming to him and saying, 'Grant me justice against my opponent.' For a while he refused; but later he said to himself, 'Though I have no fear of God and no respect for anyone, yet because this widow keeps bothering me, I will grant her justice, so that she may not wear me out by continually coming.'" And the Lord said, "Listen to what the unjust judge says. And will not God grant justice to his chosen ones who cry to him day and night?"

Luke 18:1-7

Reflection

Were you at first strangely embarrassed, dear Lord, if I may ask, when you saw your mother elbowing her way through the spectators on the Via Dolorosa, defying the soldiers' emphatic orders to back off? She disregarded their shouts as if she were a Roman matriarch. Were you, just for a moment, back at the school gates in Nazareth, feeling a bit awkward through mama's mettle? She is not going to back down, is she, any more than the persistent widow in your parable would yield to the judge's refusal to grant her access?

As you press your face into your mother's, the blood from your wounded head runs unheeded down your face. When you withdraw from the embrace, her right cheek casts back the profile of your wounds: mother mirrors her wounded son, as she always did, as indeed mothers always do. She struggles for a word, any word that might support a splinter of the weight your shoulders carry. She finds none.

Sure, her eyes have some light in them at seeing you, but the twilight prevails as she sees the condition of you. Those eyes that had trembled and rejoiced in your birth, your first words, your tottering walk, how you daftly imitated Joseph around his workplace as if you were his partner, how you struggled to become the person that you believed was mysteriously inside you, how you left home to become this emerging mystery. How you left her and home, your eyes fixed on a far horizon, attracting a curious collection of misfits, none of whom, she has noticed, yearn for your presence now.

Did it ever bother you what she thought? As her son, did you ever ask for her opinion, as some sons might, on the path you chose to take, the disciples you selected, the kind of people you believed deserved your protective love, the authorities you resolved to confront? Did you ever say: "Oh Amah, tell me, what do you think?" Maybe you did; for sure I don't know.

You know, she always imagined the reverse of this scene, that you would attend her as she was approaching death, that you would appear alone, just by yourself, without your strange friends, and sit with her and gather her in your arms and speak the gentle words you always spoke to strangers, but this time you would speak them to her, flesh of your flesh, until she finally went from your embrace to the embrace of your God and her God.

While death is a sure appointment for all of us, no mother expects to outlive her child; no mother expects to hold the body of her expiring son in her arms: she can tender no comfort, whisper no lullabies and offer no healing kiss that might be felt to make a difference. Her child's absence will define her life for ever.

In your final embrace, did your beloved mother remember how the old prophet Simeon cautioned her that day in the Temple, so long ago, that her heart would be broken in two? "This child is destined to be a sign that will be rejected," he declared. Then he leaned over to your mother and whispered: "And a sword will pierce your own soul too."

Imagine any mother hearing that annunciation of her son's future and her own. Every mother's nightmare that, for all her love, she will be sorely wounded, a dagger thrust through her very soul. Of course, as was her habit, your mother kept this to herself all these years because she had no mind, like so many mothers, to worry you or hurt you.

So here you are, the two of you, mother and son, prophecy fulfilled. In this last embrace two thoughts collide: a mother's longing for the safety of her son over against the certainty of the destiny you have chosen.

Impatient with the delay, the soldiers pull her off you, pushing her back into the crowd. You watch her go; she never looks back as your eyes carry her until she disappears into the crush of bystanders. Perhaps only now you wonder how your choices might have wounded her.

The protesting mothers

President Isabel Perón of Argentina was deposed by the military junta in 1976 and during the years of the dictatorship that lasted until 1983, more than 30,000 people were abducted by agents of the government. Many of the dissenters were young people and students trying to express their dissatisfaction with the regime. The military junta was determined to annihilate – by kidnap, interrogation and torture – not just people they judged subversive but their friends and family. The kidnapped people became referred to as *los desaparecidos*, the Spanish for "the disappeared".

This legion of the lost – students, writers and many ordinary civilians – have yet to be accounted for, and are presumed dead. During those years some five hundred expectant mothers were kidnapped and kept alive long enough to give birth; their babies were then taken away and given to families of high-ranking military officers and their colleagues. The children, of course, have been brought up without knowing their true identity.

For over thirty years, mothers of the disappeared have campaigned to have their loved ones returned. Every Thursday, at 3 p.m., a group of these determined women, many of them now grandmothers, march on the Plaza de Mayo in Buenos Aires, in front of the presidential palace, to seek justice for their families. The women wear white headscarves embroidered with the names of their loved ones.

These women tell their stories of stolen motherhood and continue to protest; like Jesus' persistent widow, they refuse to be denied justice. One of the mothers, María del Rosario de Cerruti, eloquently stated her case:

> One of the things that I simply will not do now is shut up. The women of my generation in Latin America have been taught that the man is always in charge and the woman is silent even in the face of injustice… Now I know that we have to speak out about the injustices publicly. If not, we are accomplices.

Prayer

O Lord, you search me and you know me,
you know my resting and my rising,
you discern my purpose from afar.
You mark when I walk or lie down,
all my ways lie open to you.

O where can I go from your spirit,
or where can I flee from your face?
If I climb the heavens, you are there.
If I lie in the grave, you are there.

If I take the wings of the dawn
and dwell at the sea's furthest end,
even there your hand would lead me,
your right hand would hold me fast.

If I say: "Let the darkness hide me
and the light around me be night,"
even darkness is not dark for you
and the night is as clear as the day.

For it was you who created my being,
knit me together in my mother's womb.
I thank you for the wonder of my being,
for the wonders of all your creation.

From Psalm 139

THE FIFTH STATION

Simon of Cyrene
helps Jesus
carry the cross

Scripture

They compelled a passer-by, who was coming in from the country, to carry his cross; it was Simon of Cyrene, the father of Alexander and Rufus. Then they brought Jesus to the place called Golgotha (which means the place of a skull).

Mark 15:21-22

As they led him away, they seized a man, Simon of Cyrene, who was coming from the country, and they laid the cross on him, and made him carry it behind Jesus.

Luke 23:26

Cyrene is in North Africa, originally a Greek colony. In 96 BC Cyrenaica came under Roman rule and in 67 BC was united with Crete to form a senatorial province, with Cyrene as its capital. It was mostly Greek-speaking and had a substantial Jewish population. Cyrene is now an archaeological site on the north-eastern coast of Libya. The name "Simon" is from the Hebrew *Šim'ôn*, which means "he has heard".

Reflection

It is not, dear Lord, your leading apostle, Simon bar-Jonah, who helps you carry your cross but a passing stranger, Simon from Cyrene. Simon bar-Jonah has fled with the remainder of your disciples, probably returning north to the shelter of Galilee, where they will all, most likely, reclaim their old identity as fishermen and their old direction of trawling the lake – exactly what you summoned them to leave behind them not too long ago. Now you are no longer the one who leads them but the one who is being led away by the Roman guards.

While your principal apostle makes for anonymity, Simon of Cyrene emerges from the safety of obscurity as a Jewish African, probably a pilgrim to Jerusalem, with his two sons Alexander and Rufus, to celebrate the annual feast of Passover. An innocent abroad, his religious pilgrimage is rudely interrupted when he happens on your procession to death. His appearance in your story is wholly coincidental: he has been catapulted into history, like Pontius Pilate and Herod Antipas and so many others, because he happened to meet you.

You know, of course, that Simon was not invited to help you but was compelled, seized, put upon; not a volunteer but a conscript. You are not afraid of losing face or ashamed of being helped or, indeed, disappointed that your challenge to your disciples to carry their own cross is something that you cannot now manage alone. As you have always fought to attend to the weakness and fragility of others, it comes as no surprise that you need others to attend to yours. This, you know, is part of every human story.

I suspect, dear Lord, you feel embarrassed that Simon is being treated like a slave in front of his two sons. It is their first lesson in witnessing a brutal military authority intervening in their lives, one that assumes there is no power on earth to contest its dictates. This story, sadly, continues to be told around the world.

Simon moves in obediently behind you, to follow you; you glance back with a look of gratitude, hoping he might register your thanks. As he shoulders your burden, you feel a huge weight suddenly lifting from you and then you realise that he is deliberately bearing most of the load: the cross barely rests on your right shoulder. Whatever happened to Simon, he has moved from being compelled to being compassionate, from being a passer-by to being a participant. This stranger's generosity astonishes you, and you are reminded of a parable you told, the Good Samaritan, when you wanted to astonish your hearers in telling the tale of the rank outsider who moves in to save the victim. How often your fictional stories come around to being too true to life.

As you trudge wordlessly on, the two of you try to find a rhythm in your footfall, a temperate measure for the road ahead. You try not to think about what awaits you, focusing on the demands of the present moment, trudge by faltering trudge. You have trouble seeing anything but you hear the scoffing crowd as they show their relish that someone is paying a price for the mess we all get ourselves into; you hear low murmurs of pity and prayer from a few of the onlookers; you hear your own heartbeat pulsing loudly; you hear Simon behind you take deep breaths in time with his steps.

The gathering clouds pass overhead with impunity, seeing nothing. Farther down the road, people happening on the procession might think they see two apprehended criminals bearing the weight of a shared cross.

Helping others

After leaving their punctured inflatable boat, which carried them from North Africa, a migrant carries his two children and heads for the safety of dry land. The father ploughs through the water and arrives on the Greek island of Lesbos. The weight he carries is his delight, his son and daughter, as he smiles with relief on reaching the sanctuary of land. His children have been so frightened for so long that he has to kneel down on the beach and, ever so gently, unpick the tight grasp of their fingers from around his neck before releasing them. They were one body; now they are three again.

This story has been re-enacted thousands of times as mothers and fathers have snatched their children and fled their bombed-out homes in search of safety and shelter – anywhere, but away. When your own home place becomes a death zone, like it was for the Jewish Holy Family in Judaea making their escape to their age-old enemies in Egypt, you will hardly be fussy about the people who will reach out to you in hospitality and lift that weight off your shoulders. It is unlikely you will be edgy or disparaging about your hosts' religion, their race, their colour or their nationality.

Desperation can make old enemies suddenly redundant.

Kindness has no borders and speaks in many tongues.

While some people are dedicated to punishing those who differ from them in religion or behaviour or whatever, there are many more people, thankfully, who recognise the fundamental human connection, realising that there is no "them" but only "us" in the human story.

There are many Simons in our world who surprise themselves in assisting not only vulnerable strangers but defenceless members of their own family and neighbours. There is a vast legion of people in every country who, day in and day out, tend and nurse and wash and lift those who cannot bear the weight of their burdens alone. They have an unlikely patron in Simon of Cyrene.

Prayer

O God of love, whose compassions fail not:
we bring before you the suffering of all mankind;
the necessities of the homeless;
the plight of refugees;
the sighing of prisoners;
the pains of those sick and injured;
the sorrows of the bereaved;
the fragility of the aged and infirm;
the anxiety of all who are passing through
the valley of the shadows.

Almighty and merciful God,
you who are afflicted in the affliction of your people,
comfort and relieve all of them
according to their several needs and your great mercy;
for the sake of your Son and our saviour Jesus Christ.

After St Anselm

THE SIXTH STATION

Veronica
wipes the face
of Jesus

Scripture

One of the Pharisees asked Jesus to eat with him, and he went into the Pharisee's house and took his place at the table. And a woman in the city, who was a sinner, having learned that he was eating in the Pharisee's house, brought an alabaster jar of ointment. She stood behind him at his feet, weeping, and began to bathe his feet with her tears and to dry them with her hair. Then she continued kissing his feet and anointing them with the ointment. Now when the Pharisee who had invited him saw it, he said to himself, "If this man were a prophet, he would have known who and what kind of woman this is who is touching him – that she is a sinner." Jesus spoke up and said to him, "Simon, I have something to say to you." "Teacher," he replied, "speak." "A certain creditor had two debtors; one owed five hundred denarii, and the other fifty. When they could not pay, he cancelled the debts for both of them. Now which of them will love him more?" Simon answered, "I suppose the one for whom he cancelled the greater debt." And Jesus said to him, "You have judged rightly." Then turning towards the woman, he said to Simon, "Do you see this woman? I entered your house; you gave me no water for my feet, but she has bathed my feet with her tears and dried them with her hair. You gave me no kiss, but from the time I came in she has not stopped kissing my feet. You did not anoint my head with oil, but she has anointed my feet with ointment. Therefore, I tell you, her sins, which were many, have been forgiven; hence she has shown great love. But the one to whom little is forgiven, loves little." Then he said to her, "Your sins are forgiven." But those who were at the table with him began to say among themselves, "Who is this who even forgives sins?" And he said to the woman, "Your faith has saved you; go in peace."

Luke 7:36-50

Reflection

When the woman emerges from the crowd, carrying a spotless white muslin cloth, you recognise her immediately, dear Lord: you have met her already up in Galilee when you were guest of honour at the villa of Simon the Pharisee. She caused an extraordinary sensation when she entered the all-male dining room from the atrium, passed everyone else and stopped behind you. All the blathering ceased around the table, moving into breathless silence.

She did not break the silence as she never uttered a word; she spoke through the language of her body as she started to cry when she was close to you. Her tears fell on your feet as you leaned into the table on the couch – so many tears fell that she bathed your feet with them. Then she went down on her knees and used her long loose hair as a towel to dry your feet. Not finished, she poured the perfume she had especially brought for you and covered your feet with kisses. This woman was all body language. This was the original foot-washing.

Everyone around the table had a sudden loss of appetite; you remember the scandal it caused. Every person in the room knew she was an accomplished public sinner, driven, dedicated and shameless: she was a disease that would infect anyone she touched. They were all appalled at you because you allowed her to continue with her attentions rather than scream, "Get this woman out of here!" You defended her over against the cool rectitude of Simon and ensured everyone knew whose side you were on. That was very dangerous: to prefer the attentions of a street woman to the propriety of a leading Pharisee. You are now paying the price for your strange alliances.

As she was the only person in your public ministry who ever came prepared to minister to you, you gave her the wonderful compliment that she had shown great love. You let her go in peace, assuring her that her many sins were forgiven her.

Dear Lord, you have this predictable habit of standing beside the victim because you think that all victims can do with some form of allegiance and you refused to join that hostile moral majority around that table. She never forgot that, this Veronica, and now she comes to stand beside you because you have become the victim in need of a little allegiance and help. She comes to attend you again.

The soldiers see what Veronica is about to do as she approaches with the open cloth which she carries in her two hands as if it were a delicate piece of porcelain. The soldiers look to the centurion, who decides not to stop her: he notices that your face is dribbling blood and sweat, blinding you for the road ahead, and he needs you able enough to last the journey to crucifixion. A little gentleness is permitted, he reckons, if it serves the ultimate brutality and humiliation. He signals her to pass through the guards.

Your eyes meet in easy recognition. Neither of you speaks as she gently presses the muslin cloth into the contours of your face, gently massaging your broken cheeks as she does so. Red presses through the cloth. For a moment you think this is a burial cloth as it covers your countenance but you call yourself back to the present moment and the present kindness. Your head falls forward; in a fluent gesture she adjusts the cloth so you can rest on it like a pillow in her cupped hands.

What relief you feel. You want to rest here for ever.

She is unhurried, totally present to you, unbothered about the shouting and the taunts and the madness that surround you both; for a moment it is as if the two of you are the only two people in the world. She waits until you raise your head as you try to manage a smile amidst the swelling and blisters. The centurion signals enough, dismisses her, and she takes her leave, walking backwards as if leaving the presence of a king.

As she departs, she looks at her muslin cloth to see a perfect image of your face impressed there. You know, more importantly, that it is not the cloth but her that is a true icon of you.

Tending the broken body of Jesus

St Teresa of Calcutta, better known as Mother Teresa, had her heart recruited by Jesus for her ministry to suffering people. On 10 September 1946, during the train ride from Calcutta to Darjeeling, Teresa received her "call within a call". On that day, in a way she would never explain, Jesus' thirst for the most vulnerable people took hold of her heart.

The parable of Jesus that dominated her life was the last judgement where people are welcomed as "blessed of my Father" because they paid attention to the legion of those in need within their reach. Six categories of people in distress are listed, together with six appropriate responses.

Those who are vulnerable

"I"
- the hungry
- the thirsty
- the stranger
- the naked
- the sick
- the imprisoned

Those who pay attention

"You"
- give food
- give drink
- offer welcome
- clothe
- visit
- go to see

In the left-hand column there is a list of vulnerable human beings whose needs await recognition and help, together with the startling revelation that Jesus' real presence abides among them. In the right-hand column there is a list of humane responses by good people, together with the startling revelation that Jesus himself was the beneficiary of these kindnesses. Misery obliged these loving people to act; their response was humane and, therefore, profoundly religious; they are celebrated for tending the broken body of Jesus.

Jesus focuses attention on his continuing presence among those who are needy: his "I" is ever present among people in need. It is as if Jesus deliberately turns us away from an exclusive focus on himself, challenging us to look elsewhere to find him. In so doing, he inspires us to face the pain and loss endured by others, not keep staring at him. He will be found where others suffer.

If there is one person who illustrated the beauty of this Gospel truth it is the sainted Mother Teresa.

Prayer

Look with compassion, O Lord,
upon the earth that is marred by darkness and cruelty.
Look with pity on all the peoples
on whom have fallen the miseries of war.

Have mercy on the wounded and the dying;
comfort those who are broken-hearted;
assuage the madness of oppressors
and deliver those who are persecuted.

We commend to you, O Lord,
all who suffer in time of war and terror:
the homeless, the wounded, the sick,
the hungry, the anxious and the frightened.

When people's liberty is lost to the oppressor,
let not their spirit and hope be broken.
May all peoples be brought through strife to contentment
and the nations of the world be united in lasting peace.

This we pray to the one who was imprisoned,
the one who was stripped bare and executed:
Jesus Christ our Lord.

THE SEVENTH STATION

Jesus falls the second time

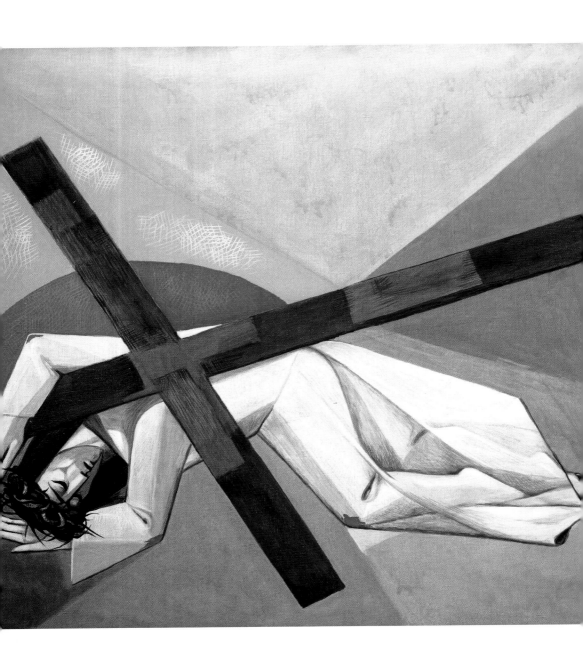

Scripture

They went to a place called Gethsemane; and he said to his disciples, "Sit here while I pray." He took with him Peter and James and John, and began to be distressed and agitated. And he said to them, "I am deeply grieved, even to death; remain here, and keep awake." And going a little farther, he threw himself on the ground and prayed that, if it were possible, the hour might pass from him. He said, "Abba, Father, for you all things are possible; remove this cup from me; yet, not what I want, but what you want." He came and found them sleeping; and he said to Peter, "Simon, are you asleep? Could you not keep awake one hour? Keep awake and pray that you may not come into the time of trial; the spirit indeed is willing, but the flesh is weak." And again he went away and prayed, saying the same words. And once more he came and found them sleeping, for their eyes were very heavy; and they did not know what to say to him. He came a third time and said to them, "Are you still sleeping and taking your rest? Enough! The hour has come; the Son of Man is betrayed into the hands of sinners. Get up, let us be going. See, my betrayer is at hand."

Mark 14:32-42

Reflection

Laid low again, dear Lord, as you were in Gethsemane: there you threw yourself on the ground, agitated and grieved about what was waiting for you beyond that olive grove. In your prayer to Abba you expressed your longing for leaving, dreaming of a quick exit, to avoid the misery of staying in place and facing the nightmare ahead. You wanted out of the waiting game, so you became a beggar, prostrate on the ground, imploring your Father to spare you and then rising to beseech your disciples to help you find an answer. But they could find no answer for you, could they?

The mighty prophet they followed for three years is now reduced to graphic vulnerability. The one who took on the religious authorities, who opposed the powers of darkness, who seemed able to take on the world – this man now looks more like a crumbling wreck. Your collapse and prayer of desperation were hardly likely to promote confidence in your disciples. Few people can hold on to the idea of leadership and vulnerability in one person; it is even more difficult when that person is you.

You decided bravely to face the approaching pain. Remember how you said to your disciples, "Get up, let us be going"? They did get up but not to follow you but to abandon you to your fate. They could make no sense of what was happening to you: the great leader they had followed was now being led away and handed over to be tortured and sentenced.

Now you hit the ground again, dear Lord. Numbed in this new fall, do you ever think you are in a dream sequence and that you'll soon wake up in bed, in the uneventful peace of Nazareth, and register with relief that it has all been a misunderstanding, a passing nightmare? Lying there dazed, do you dream that you might soon come round to a new morning, realising that there are no soldiers hovering, no fear of another whiplash, no cross on your back, only a cockcrow outside your door – one that does not accuse anyone but heralds a new day?

The numbness wears off, too soon, and you come back to yourself, to the present moment and its wretched, undeniable reality. The road awaits you for a walk that is like no other you've taken – not a wander around your home village, not a stroll by the Sea of Galilee, not a welcome saunter north to Tyre and Sidon with your disciples to get away from all the bother of crowds pressing in with their demands. No, this is it, the final journey.

You feel a sharp pain in your shoulder; you lie stock-still, hoping the stillness might dismiss it or at least decrease the intensity. The throbbing is not going to go away magically, you know, so better to get up and move on.

While you strain to regain your pace, you grow weary, dear Lord, not only from the journey but from the intensity of cool looks, the curiosity of those who pass by and some others who decide to attend the drama as spectators. Startled eyes stare. It's as if they have nothing better to do than to inspect the details of wreckage. Do they want to fondle your scars, to test they are real?

Why, you wonder, are people so fascinated with the misfortune of others? Why do they slow their pace, even loiter, at a scene of disaster? Out there, beyond themselves, someone or something is crumbling. Does it make them feel better, luckier, more blessed that they can move on their way, feeling more secure? Or do they pause and say: "There but for the grace of God go I"?

Who knows, dear Lord?

A cavalcade of Roman nobility passes by, horses' hooves clattering on the stones, chariot wheels whipping up dust as the column hurries to Herod's palace, now the official residence of the Roman governor. This disturbance, usefully, diverts people's attention for a few moments, but only for a few: vulnerability, it has to be said, is more interesting than majesty; real human affliction more gripping than passing ceremonial, so the attention reverts to you.

Business as usual

In January 2012, the Italian cruise liner *Costa Concordia* sailed too close to the Tuscan island of Giglio and hit a large rock which made a fifty-metre gash in the ship's port side below the waterline. The ship started listing and then fell heavily into the sea, killing thirty-two people. At the beginning of this special voyage, the passengers and crew were looking forward to a peaceful Mediterranean cruise: tragedy interrupted.

Suffering happens in the midst of an ordinary day or a special day; the sun shines indiscriminately on the living and the dying; tragedy takes place while people are having a cup of tea or taking the dog for a walk. Bombs fall on the school while children struggle with arithmetic lessons; two boys playing football on the beach are dematerialised by a missile. Ordinary life is the theatre of suffering and loss. That observation is caught beautifully in Brueghel's painting and underlined in the sharp commentary by the poet W.H. Auden.

> *Musée des Beaux Arts*
> About suffering they were never wrong,
> The old Masters: how well they understood
> Its human position: how it takes place
> While someone else is eating or opening a window
> or just walking dully along…
>
> In Brueghel's Icarus, for instance: how everything turns away
> Quite leisurely from the disaster; the ploughman may
> Have heard the splash, the forsaken cry,
> But for him it was not an important failure; the sun shone
> As it had to on the white legs disappearing into the green
> Water, and the expensive delicate ship that must have seen
> Something amazing, a boy falling out of the sky,
> Had somewhere to get to and sailed calmly on.[3]

Life goes on in the course of others' personal disaster. As Seamus Heaney observed: "Passive suffering makes the world go round."

Prayer

Batter my heart, three-person'd God, for you
As yet but knock, breathe, shine, and seek to mend;
That I may rise and stand, o'erthrow me, and bend
Your force to break, blow, burn, and make me new.
I, like an usurp'd town to another due,
Labour to admit you, but oh, to no end;
Reason, your viceroy in me, me should defend,
But is captiv'd, and proves weak or untrue.
Yet dearly I love you, and would be lov'd fain,
But am betroth'd unto your enemy;
Divorce me, untie or break that knot again,
Take me to you, imprison me, for I,
Except you enthrall me, never shall be free,
Nor ever chaste, except you ravish me.

John Donne,
Holy Sonnets, XIV

THE EIGHTH STATION

Jesus meets the women of Jerusalem

Scripture

A great number of the people followed him, and among them were women who were beating their breasts and wailing for him. But Jesus turned to them and said, "Daughters of Jerusalem, do not weep for me, but weep for yourselves and for your children. For the days are surely coming when they will say, 'Blessed are the barren, and the wombs that never bore, and the breasts that never nursed.' Then they will begin to say to the mountains, 'Fall on us'; and to the hills, 'Cover us.' For if they do this when the wood is green, what will happen when it is dry?"

Luke 23:27-31

Reflection

You glance over your shoulder, dear Lord, to see who is following you now, still hopeful that you can spot a stray disciple straggling behind at a cautious distance. But no. You notice this, of course, how can you not? Since you called them this is the first journey you have taken without them following behind you. Their large absence is noticed also by the monitoring soldiers: the centurion has briefed them that it is extremely unlikely there will be protests from your male followers since the governor's spies informed him that your chosen ones have already disappeared north to Galilee. The intelligence service reckons that none of them would pose a threat; no soldiers, therefore, would be commanded to hunt them down.

Instead of your disciples a group of women openly share their grief at what is happening to you. You know well that suffering can embarrass some people: they don't know what to say and stay away or they can feel repelled rather than moved by the torment before their eyes; they can find it all aesthetically displeasing, a nuisance, in their world of refinement. Neither these women of Jerusalem nor their children are distant or repelled as they express their sorrow for your plight.

Why is it that it is only women who, without being asked, reach out to you on the Via Dolorosa?

Are you surprised, dear Lord? Why is it that so many women turn up in painful places, attentive to the plight of the wretched? They refuse to remain as neutral observers, unmoved movers, apathetic in the face of tragedy. They express their solidarity with you as they beat their breasts and wail loudly. One of my teachers, Dorothee Sölle, expressed it passionately in her book *Suffering*:

> When you look at human suffering concretely, you destroy all innocence, all neutrality, every attempt to say, "It wasn't I; there was nothing I could do; I didn't know." In the face of suffering you are either with the victim or the executioner – there is no other option.[4]

These women have bravely chosen which side they are on: they are with you, the victim. Moving away from your own suffering, however, you reach out to them in compassion and share your concern for their future heartache as women of this particular city: daughters of Jerusalem. You tell them their tears are better shed for themselves and for their children. It's as if you say, dear Lord, that your individual suffering is nothing compared to the shared affliction that awaits them all.

In the Beatitudes you blessed those who mourned and now you offer a strange saying:

> For the days are surely coming when they will say, "Blessed are the barren, and the wombs that never bore, and the breasts that never nursed."

Given that barren wombs were always regarded as a curse, why would people be led to bless them? What events will happen when mothers will be relieved they have no children to worry about, no offspring to agonise about their fate? Will the coming revolt against Rome and the inevitable vicious suppression be such a tortured time that mothers will bless God they have no sons or daughters to swell the litany of victims?

You predict the city's destruction, warning that the Romans will inflict such debasement and destruction on them that they will beg the mountains to fall on them and bury them as a fate preferable to enduring the expert brutal attention of their oppressors. You say: "For if they do this when the wood is green, what will happen when it is dry?" If in peacetime your innocence is abused and assaulted so severely, what will happen to those who oppose the power of Rome?

On your own Via Dolorosa, in the midst of your own suffering, you are mindful, dear Lord, to alert the women to the approaching time when they will surely walk their own way of sorrows. You know this road is not peculiar to you but will be crowded throughout history with victims enduring their own struggle and heading for their own death.

We pray that someone might notice them, attend them and grieve for them.

The mourning women

They had exhausted themselves, waiting and weeping, following the mine disaster in Soma, Turkey, on 13 May 2014. Coal had been the main industry in their home town for decades with its attendant dangers and daily fears. The women – wives, mothers, grandmothers, sisters, girlfriends – all gathered, chanting the names of their lost ones, each hoping madly for the best outcome but sadly expecting the worst.

An explosion at the coal mine in Soma caused an underground mine fire, which burned for two days and nights. The fire occurred at the mine's shift change, and 787 workers were underground at the time of the explosion. In total, 301 people were killed in what was the worst mine disaster in Turkey's history.

Like many women before them, they turned up to a scene of disaster to wait, to watch, to wonder at the arrived calamity, to pray and to find some wee comfort in their shared pain and loss.

They did not have to put themselves in the others' shoes to sympathise: they were all wearing the same shoes.

Soon the grieving relatives had to lay their loved ones to rest in mass burials as gravediggers laboured overtime to provide more space for more victims. Whatever our dreams, often real life interrupts: too often everything happens so quickly.

Women wailed loudly, swaying and singing laments about the departed as their bodies were lowered, one by one, into the freshly dug graves. Forty-five-year-old Gulizar Donmez, whose husband and father were both miners, said: "The wives of the miners kiss their husbands in the morning. If they are late back from work, even by five minutes, everyone starts calling. You never know what is going to happen."

"You never know what is going to happen" is the responsorial to so many daily psalms that people make in hard times.

Later on, too soon, so many of these women would weep for themselves and for their children.

Prayer

Thy way, not mine, O Lord,
However dark it be!
Lead me by thine own hand,
Choose out the path for me;
Smooth let it be or rough,
It will be still the best;
Winding or straight, it leads
Right onward to thy rest.

The kingdom that I seek
Is thine; so let the way
That leads to it be thine,
Else I must surely stray.
I dare not choose my lot;
I would not if I might:
Choose thou for me, my God,
So shall I walk aright.

Take thou my cup, and it
With joy or sorrow fill
As best to thee may seem;
Choose thou my good and ill.
Not mine, not mine the choice
In things or great or small;
Be thou my guide, my strength,
My wisdom, and my all.

Horatius Bonar

THE NINTH STATION

Jesus falls
the third time

Scripture

All we like sheep have gone astray;
we have all turned to our own way,
and the Lord has laid on him
the iniquity of us all.

He was oppressed, and he was afflicted,
yet he did not open his mouth;
Like a lamb that is led to the slaughter,
and like a sheep that before its shearers is silent…

Out of his anguish he shall see light;
he shall find satisfaction through his knowledge.
The righteous one, my servant, shall make many righteous,
and he shall bear their iniquities.

Therefore I will allot him a portion with the great,
and he shall divide the spoil with the strong;
because he poured out himself to death,
and was numbered with the transgressors;
yet he bore the sin of many,
and made intercession for the transgressors.

Isaiah 53:6-7. 11-12

Reflection

After passing through the huge limestone arch of the city gate, you set your face, dear Lord, for the short journey to Golgotha. The city of Jerusalem that you wept over silently witnesses your departure. You hear your own breath labouring in and out of your body; your feet feel sticky on the rough stones; the ground seems to be sliding away from you and you stop to gather what little strength you have left. You notice how people are coming in and going out of the city gate: this is the road that leads south to Bethlehem, the place of your birth. But you will not head down this road again; your destination is nearby, the killing fields of Golgotha, a disused quarry.

As you see the destination that awaits you, you collapse under the weight of the view ahead. Your energy is spent; your mind numbed; your body feels like a useless broken vessel that can no longer obey your commands. Your feet refuse to anchor you any longer: as you fall down again, it feels as if this time the ground rises up to thump you senseless.

Prostrate again, you long to close your eyes and drift into an endless sleep. Instead you decide to stay stubbornly attentive – how much time have you left, after all? – and look up at the people pressing their way through the gate. Their outlines are somewhat blurred by the mixture of sweat and blood you try to blink away, but you allow each passing face to imprint itself on your consciousness for a moment.

A mother covers the eyes of her curious twin sons and pushes them blindly onwards. A farmer wheels a rickety barrow to the market – apricots and figs are almost covered with an old tattered cloth, to prevent people from helping themselves as they rush past. You hear an old man, his eyes fixed on some far horizon, mutter to his legs to keep going: you almost smile in sympathy with him. An agitated man is holding forth outside the city gate about the unfairness of the poll tax with an audience of only two soldiers.

Most people ignore the spectacle at hand and hurry on their way: life goes on. Where before you were always noticed and attended to, dear Lord, now all this seems to have faded as people go about their business. You are just another condemned criminal outside the only gate that leads to the place of execution; you are an all-too-familiar sight in this place; invisibility has crept up on you, like so many people who suffer. One of your admirers will later write about you as the stranger from heaven:

> He was in the world, and the world came into being through him; yet the world did not know him. He came to what was his own, and his own people did not accept him.

You wonder for a moment about your disciples, hoping they are safe, wherever they are. You knew they could not follow you on this road, dear Lord, and you warned them in the graveyard of the Kidron Valley that they would all abandon you. Peter protested, shouting out in the graveyard that he would never desert you. "Never", he howled. You hope he is not covered now in his own shame. How could they follow you now, exposed and vulnerable to everything people want to do to you?

You seem, dear Lord, to have lost the habit of being in control. When most of us think of leadership we often think of it in terms of control and authority and power. People expect you as the shepherd to go in front and show the way, to lead, while others follow your direction. Now, as you predicted, the time has come when the shepherd is struck down and the sheep are scattered.

The soldiers step in, reckoning that you have given yourself enough of an unscheduled break, pulling you upright and reuniting you with your burden, placing it back on your shoulders. You struggle upright, keeping your eyes fixed on the heavens. You notice the clouds seem to be hurrying ahead of you as if impatient, before having a last fling towards darkness. Not long to go now; the place of execution beckons.

The fall of the Twin Towers

On that day, Tuesday 11 September 2001, we observers entered a dreamlike state: we thought we saw this before, on disaster films with special effects – the explosions, the red flames and black clouds, the crowds running through the streets. But this was not virtual reality; this was real.

We saw an image of passion – of people being acted upon without their consent; of innocents becoming the objects of other people's cruel intentions. We saw the two planes being aimed at the World Trade Center where thousands of people worked; the dreadful impact; the red explosions; the dust engulfing the streets into darkness. But it was what we could not see that was truly frightening. We were left to imagine the human terror inside the planes, in the corridors and the lobbies and the elevators of the stricken buildings. We were left to imagine the horror in the streets below as the buildings later collapsed on firefighters and police officers and helpers.

The real terror we witnessed was offstage, out of view. In their tragedies the Greeks kept their worst moments of terror offstage because they were too offensive to put on view: this is the original meaning of the word "obscene". We did not see the real obscenity: what was really repulsive happened away from our sight. We were watching death on a vast scale, but we saw no one die. We watched people waving helplessly from windows, but we did not hear their screams. We watched people jump from high windows, but saw no bodies hit the ground. Watching this tragedy made some of us feel like tourists at the crucifixion. The horror was at a safe remove.

That passion story, sadly, continues to be told. We pray for all people who are abused and tortured and dismissed into death. May their names be held holy before the Lord.

Prayer

You have taken away my friends
and made me hateful in their sight.
Imprisoned, I cannot escape;
my eyes are sunken with grief.

I call to you, Lord, all the day long;
to you I stretch out my hands.
Will you work your wonders for the dead?
Will the shades stand and praise you?

Will your love be told in the grave
or your faithfulness among the dead?
Will your wonders be known in the dark
or your justice in the land of oblivion?

As for me, Lord, I call to you for help;
in the morning my prayer comes before you.
Lord, why do you reject me?
Why do you hide your face?

Wretched, close to death from my youth,
I have borne your trials; I am numb.
Your fury has swept down upon me;
your terrors have utterly destroyed me.

They surround me all the day like a flood,
they assail me all together.
Friend and neighbour you have taken away:
my one companion is darkness.

From Psalm 88

THE TENTH STATION

Jesus is stripped of his garments

Scripture

They tear holes in my hands and my feet
and lay me in the dust of death.

I can count every one of my bones.
These people stare at me and gloat;
they divide my clothing among them.
They cast lots for my robe.

O Lord, do not leave me alone,
my strength, make haste to help me!

From Psalm 22

All of them deserted him and fled.

A certain young man was following him, wearing nothing but a linen cloth. They caught hold of him, but he left the linen cloth and ran off naked.

Mark 14:50-52

Reflection

When you called your first disciples by the lake of Galilee, dear Lord, they were busy in their boats mending the splits in their nets. On hearing your call, they immediately dropped their nets to follow you, leaving not only their trade but their families behind them, to attach themselves to you. They did not abandon their world of the familiar because you had outlined a challenging mission that would await them; they left everything to follow you. They went after *you* – not an idea, not a project, not a missionary programme. It was all very personal.

How things have changed… In the olive grove of Gethsemane, when the arresting party tried to get hold of the young disciple who was wearing only a linen cloth, he was so desperate to get away from all the disruption and the shouting and your arrest that he left his laundry in their hands and ran away naked. How things have changed… Now the disciple will drop everything in order to get away from you.

How do we stay attached to what first attracted us?

It is now time for you to be publicly stripped of your garments. This, as you know, is an important part of the degrading ritual that precedes crucifixion: after being scourged, the prisoner must make the tortuous journey of carrying his cross; on reaching the place of execution he is publicly humiliated further by being stripped naked by the soldiers. Whatever dignity you had left is now stripped away, leaving your exposed broken body for all to see.

How must you feel, dear Lord? You are made into a cruel public exhibition, street theatre, entertainment for the crowds. Some onlookers, it has to be said, adjust their position for a better view, to inspect the details of shame.

Modesty is an important virtue in your Jewish tradition, I know, right from the time of Adam and Eve who covered their nakedness from each other after eating of the tree of knowledge. Ever since, covering up modestly has been the normal practice, respecting our own and other people's right to the privacy of our bodies, our personal territory. Of course, perversely, that has enticed others to invade that personal enclosure, trespass on its privacy and violate its integrity.

Wherever there is a sanctuary, there will always be iconoclasts.

You will remember that one day you spoke to your disciples of your body as temple, as sacred space, as sanctuary, as shelter. One of your followers will later describe the body as a temple of the Holy Spirit: that, surely, is especially true of yours. Now your temple is dishonoured, defiled, desecrated. You stand there on Golgotha, the place of the skull, naked: the authorities want your life, not knowing that you handed it over a long time ago.

But I love you for this, dear Lord: although subjected to this indecency of being stripped naked to public view, you do not feel indecent, do you? You know that the offensive acts assailants perform on innocent people do not make the victims indecent or dirty or impure, something the violators always try to contrive. They hope that they can transfer the wrong, that their intrusion will be owned by the victim, making the victim feel the blame for this outrage.

But innocence remains innocence and remains innocent no matter how it is assailed or abused: guilt does not transplant itself to the victim.

Of course, as a condemned criminal you have no rights, no dignity and no respect. You have no higher court to appeal to in Judaea; you are not a Roman citizen, only – as the authorities see you – a rustic from the highlands of Galilee, a man of no importance.

I know you worry how your mother must see all this: certainly your nakedness does not surprise her, but this act of diminishment must shock her. As you look at yourself through her eyes, you hear the echo of an ancient voice: "This child is destined to be rejected."

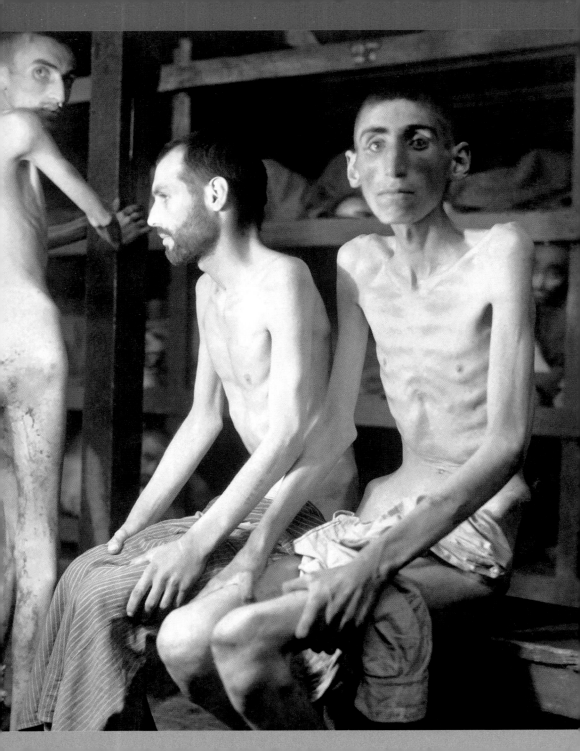

Stripped bare

How do you humiliate and destroy the psyche of a captive? Abu Ghraib prison in Iraq was used as a detention centre in 2003: stigmatised groups were dehumanised and placed beyond the boundary in which moral values, convention and concern for justice apply. Among the abuses that were listed by a United States Army report were:

- forcing detainees to remove their clothing and keep them naked for several hours or days;

- punching, slapping and kicking naked detainees;

- placing a dog chain or strap around a naked detainee's neck and having a soldier drag the crawling prisoner along the corridors of the cells.

Most of the abuse centred on the prisoners being naked, stripped of even the minimal covering. Similar methods were used in Auschwitz concentration camp. In the last book he wrote before his death, *The Drowned and the Saved*, Primo Levi shared his experience of being a prisoner in Auschwitz and of "the coercion of nudity" that was regularly used by the guards:

> Now a naked and barefoot man feels that all his nerves and tendons are severed: he is a helpless prey. Clothes, even the foul clothes which were distributed, even the crude clogs with their wooden soles, are a tenuous but indispensable defence. Anyone who does not have them no longer perceives himself as a human being, but rather as a worm: naked, slow, ignoble, prone on the ground. He knows that he can be crushed at any moment.[5]

Long before this Jewish writer spoke of feeling like a worm, two thousand years earlier one of the psalmists wrote:

> But I am a worm and no man,
> scorned by men, despised by the people.

That story of degrading people, treating them like an animal, is as modern as it is ancient. There seems to be an abiding consensus among torturers: the first step to humiliating a captive is to strip the captive bare.

Prayer

Lord Jesus,
you experienced in person torture and death
as a prisoner of conscience.
You were beaten and flogged
and sentenced to an agonising death
though you had done no wrong.

Be now with prisoners of conscience
throughout the world.
Be with them in their fear and loneliness,
in the agony of physical and mental torture
and in the face of execution and death.

Stretch out your hands in power
to break their chains.
Be merciful to the oppressor and torturer
and place a new heart within them.
Forgive all injustices in our lives
and transform us to be instruments of your peace,
for by your wounds we are healed.

Amnesty International

THE ELEVENTH STATION

Jesus is nailed
to the cross

Scripture

And when they came to a place called Golgotha (which means Place of a Skull), they offered him wine to drink, mixed with gall; but when he tasted it, he would not drink it. And when they had crucified him, they divided his clothes among themselves by casting lots; then they sat down there and kept watch over him. Over his head they put the charge against him, which read, "This is Jesus, the King of the Jews."

Then two bandits were crucified with him, one on his right and one on his left. Those who passed by derided him, shaking their heads and saying, "You who would destroy the temple and build it in three days, save yourself! If you are the Son of God, come down from the cross." In the same way the chief priests also, along with the scribes and elders, were mocking him, saying, "He saved others; he cannot save himself. He is the King of Israel; let him come down from the cross now, and we will believe in him. He trusts in God; let God deliver him now, if he wants to; for he said, 'I am God's Son.'" The bandits who were crucified with him also taunted him in the same way.

Matthew 27:33-44

Reflection

As the nails penetrate your hands and feet, dear Lord, you look up and away from the savage attention the soldiers dutifully inflict on you: they concentrate on nailing you fast to lumber. You look heavenwards: I wonder what you are wondering. I am thinking of Isaac, especially when his father Abraham placed the wood of sacrifice on his back and made him carry it up another hill – Mount Moriah – a stone's throw away from where you are laid down. Remember how Abraham laid the wood on the makeshift altar and then bound Isaac to the wood, so that he could offer his son as a sacrifice to God? A father raised a knife, ready to kill his beloved son simply because God commanded him to do it.

It has always surprised me, dear Lord, how that story never allows us entry into the agony of Isaac – whose name, strangely, signifies laughter... The agony of the son is overlooked; the daring of the father is celebrated. But why did Abraham leave his son on the altar of sacrifice and return alone to his servants? Why did he not gather his wounded son in his arms, speak gentle words and beg forgiveness for attempted filicide? How did Isaac manage as a survivor after that gruesome experience? Did he ever talk to his father again? Did he ever laugh again?

Abraham is hailed as a hero for yielding to God's heartbreaking demand. But what kind of father would be willing to kill his son to prove a point? What point is worth proving when you behold a son dead at your own hand? What kind of God would ask of a father the murder of his son? Or was Abraham testing God to see if God would go through with it?

The good news, of course, is that an angel arrives just in time to stop the human sacrifice. Are you hoping, dear Lord, as you are now bound to the wood for sacrifice, that an angel might still come, even though it is surely getting late?

What are you thinking now there is little time left to think? Are you reviewing in your head all you did and said? What did you do or say that has landed you up here? Could you have been more circumspect about your rolling attack on the religious authorities? Like John the Baptist, your great mentor, you were never raised on diplomatic niceties and had an aversion to the conditional tense. Looking back, dear Lord, would you have done anything differently?

Personally speaking, I think your passion began when you entered the synagogue in Capernaum on that sabbath day and all eyes were upon you. Remember? A man with a withered arm was sitting quietly and when he saw you, he did not scream, "Lord, have mercy." Nevertheless you provoked the ensuing conflict by ordering him to stand out in the middle and then questioned everyone else: "Is it lawful to do good or to do harm on the sabbath, to save life or to kill?" No one wanted to join your seminar, which made you grieved and angry. And when you healed the man, the Pharisees and the Herodians went out to plot how to destroy you. Their real devotions – to terminate you – began when they left sacred space. And, it has to be said, they have succeeded.

Now the soldiers hoist the cross upright and the angled uplift intensifies the pain in your hands and feet: you feel you are tearing apart as you shudder into place. The crown of thorns stabs into the back of your head as it thuds against the upright stake.

Is this where you belong, dear Lord? Is this a terrible mistake or a goal achieved? People don't head deliberately towards a mistake, do they? Mistakes are only recognised backwards. But you set your face towards this place like it was meant to be, like you had to keep an ancient appointment with death.

You look down at the assembled rabble. The soldiers who have mocked you, flogged you and crucified you now stand back, surveying their handiwork – choreographed brutality. The crowd gawps. The scorners close in with full voice.

No angel comes.

Role reversal

Bethlehem is a small city located some six miles south of the Old City of Jerusalem; it is within the West Bank, administered by the Palestinian Authority. It is revered by Jews as the birthplace and home town of David, king of Israel, and by Christians as the traditional birthplace of Jesus. In 1994, the first section of the Israeli West Bank wall was built with slabs of concrete. Today Bethlehem is a besieged city surrounded on three sides by a twenty-five-foot-high concrete wall. For the Israelis, the wall is a protection from Palestinian suicide bombers; for the Palestinians, the barrier has cut into their lands, separating them from relatives and schools and workplaces.

Banksy, an English graffiti artist and political activist, is well known for his satirical street art: his works of social criticism have appeared on streets and walls throughout the world. In 2005 Banksy created this stencilled image on the wall of the West Bank in Bethlehem, known as *Girl and a Soldier*.

It features a young girl, in pigtails, frisking an armed Israeli soldier: innocence apprehends the ruling command. The soldier is seen in the classic position of the one subjected to stop and search, his hands raised against the wall which he faces, his legs spread apart as he is patted down by the girl. You notice his rifle laid aside. Banksy selected Bethlehem for the exhibit because it is the birthplace of the Prince of Peace and because of the regular unrest between the local inhabitants and the soldiers.

The wall the soldier is leaning against symbolises the divide between the Israelis and Palestinians, a division as raw as that between the Romans and the Jews at the time of Jesus. While it is not easy to interpret Banksy's image, it is something of a warning against assuming people as hostile because of their religion or ethnicity. Every day people get hammered because they belong to the "wrong" country or colour or creed.

Prayer

My God, my God, why have you forsaken me?
You are far from my plea and the cry of my distress.
O my God, I call by day and you give no reply;
I call by night and I find no peace.

Yet you, O God, are holy,
enthroned on the praises of Israel.
In you our fathers put their trust;
they trusted and you set them free.
When they cried to you, they escaped.
In you they trusted and never in vain.

But I am a worm and no man,
scorned by men, despised by the people.
All who see me deride me.
They curl their lips, they toss their heads.
"He trusted in the Lord, let him save him;
let him release him if this is his friend."

Yes, it was you who took me from the womb,
entrusted me to my mother's breast.
To you I was committed from my birth,
from my mother's womb you have been my God.
Do not leave me alone in my distress;
come close, there is none else to help.

From Psalm 22

THE TWELFTH STATION

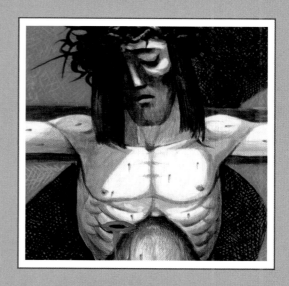

Jesus dies on
the cross

Scripture

When it was noon, darkness came over the whole land until three in the afternoon. At three o'clock Jesus cried out with a loud voice, "Eloi, Eloi, lema sabachthani?" which means, "My God, my God, why have you forsaken me?" When some of the bystanders heard it, they said, "Listen, he is calling for Elijah." And someone ran, filled a sponge with sour wine, put it on a stick, and gave it to him to drink, saying, "Wait, let us see whether Elijah will come to take him down." Then Jesus gave a loud cry and breathed his last.

Mark 15:33-37

When they came to the place that is called The Skull, they crucified Jesus there with the criminals, one on his right and one on his left. Then Jesus said, "Father, forgive them; for they do not know what they are doing"…

It was now about noon, and darkness came over the whole land until three in the afternoon, while the sun's light failed; and the curtain of the temple was torn in two. Then Jesus, crying with a loud voice, said, "Father, into your hands I commend my spirit." Having said this, he breathed his last. When the centurion saw what had taken place, he praised God and said, "Certainly this man was innocent."

Luke 23:33-34. 44-47

After this, when Jesus knew that all was now finished, he said (in order to fulfil the scripture), "I am thirsty." A jar full of sour wine was standing there. So they put a sponge full of the wine on a branch of hyssop and held it to his mouth. When Jesus had received the wine, he said, "It is finished." Then he bowed his head and gave up his spirit.

John 19:28-30

Reflection

You have kept, dear Lord, your rendezvous with death in Jerusalem. Beyond the excruciating pain you are enduring, you are finding it difficult to draw breath. The weight of your body, pulling down on your outstretched arms and shoulders, makes for your shallow breathing; the onset of muscle cramps due to fatigue hinders your breathing even further. Every breath you struggle to take seems to be your last.

As you approach death you take your last look out beyond Golgotha, south towards Bethlehem, remembering how others told you how the world had rejoiced at your birth and how peace seemed to triumph over everything, when angels were chanting, shepherds were adoring and wise men from the east unexpectedly arrived with their curious gifts. And then, without warning, all was interrupted by the sound of horses' hooves clattering on the stones at the entrance to Bethlehem as King Herod's cavalry galloped in from Jerusalem hell-bent on destruction. How everything can suddenly go wrong. So suddenly.

The soldiers missed you then. Now, however late, they have you in their hold.

You always had an educated eye for those on the margins of life and even now you notice an old man as he approaches the outskirts of the crowd to sell sweetmeats: he presses forward, appealing to everyone to buy his delicacies. You cannot but smile in your mind: funny, you think, how adversity produces entrepreneurs.

You have to endure, dear Lord, such a raw and brutal ending to a gentle life. Later your death will be written up in three ways, read from three different viewpoints.

> Is nature in sympathy with you, so that nature puts on mourning and covers the earth in darkness? Are you dying, screaming an accusation at God for abandoning you? Your request in Gethsemane was refused: "Take this cup away from me." Do you feel you have entered the ultimate darkness, that you have now been isolated inside the forsakenness of God? Is your last act a scream of protest for being stranded by God?

You set your face towards Jerusalem, knowing it was your ultimate destination. Did you die as you lived, heaping forgiveness on everything in sight? Is your last act to forgive your persecutors and assure the good thief that he will be with you in paradise? Are you dying, committing yourself in gratitude into the secure and loving hands of God?

Even more, are you dying in majesty, justifying the title above your head? You have finished the work that your Father gave you to do; you have loved to the very end those who were in the world. Do you see your life and death as a real achievement, a mission completed so that you can now, without regret, hand over your spirit and depart in peace?

I know that no observer or writer can capture every detail of a subject's life experience and dying. Who can enter the depth of your mind or heart, O Lord, and produce a living portrait that is complete? We cannot claim, two thousand years later, that we fully understand you, the most interesting and complex human being who has walked on this earth.

We do know, however, that your love for us is beyond telling, a love that makes its way with a cross on its back. We are sure of your kindness and mercy, shared in life and in death. We are secure in the belief that your death is not some catastrophic mischance devoid of meaning, but a purposeful saving act that graces our lives every day. By your wounds we are healed.

The lines of the poet Alan Seeger, who died in World War I, could have been written for you, dear Lord:

> I have a rendezvous with Death
> On some scarred slope of battered hill,
> When Spring comes round again this year
> And the first meadow-flowers appear…
>
> And I to my pledged word am true,
> I shall not fail that rendezvous. [6]

A sign of hope

From the Libyan coastal towns west of Tripoli, it is 275 miles to Sicily, 215 miles to Malta, but only 160 miles to the small Italian island of Lampedusa, off the south-east coast of Sicily. Approaching the island, on 3 October 2013, a boat was wrecked carrying refugees from Eritrea and Somalia. Over 500 people were on board when the overcrowded boat caught fire, capsized and sank. Only 151 people survived.

Some of the survivors were Eritrean Christians, fleeing persecution in their home country, and they attended the church of San Gerlando on the island. Francesco Tuccio, a carpenter and parishioner who lives on the island, met the survivors at the church and worshipped with them. He felt dismayed at not being able to make any difference to their plight. What to do? With only his woodworking skills to offer, he collected some of the wood from the wreckage that had washed up onto the beach and made each of the survivors a cross to reflect their salvation and as a symbol of hope for the future, that they might regain their dignity and freedom.

The last acquisition made by Neil MacGregor at the end of thirteen years as director of the British Museum was the Lampedusa Cross. Francesco Tuccio was commissioned to make it and he donated his cross to the museum as a symbol of the suffering and hope of our times. When the museum thanked him he wrote: "It is I who should thank you for drawing attention to the burden symbolised by this small piece of wood."

"Ave crux, unica spes" – "Hail the cross, our only hope" – comes from a stanza of an ancient Roman hymn, which dates back to the sixth century; it is traditionally sung in the Catholic liturgy of Good Friday. While it seems strange to put cross and hope together, the Lampedusa Cross celebrates exactly that mingling – made from wreckage and offered as a symbol of hope.

Prayer

If we have never sought, we seek Thee now;
Thine eyes burn through the dark, our only stars;
We must have sight of thorn-pricks on Thy brow,
We must have Thee, O Jesus of the Scars.

The heavens frighten us; they are too calm;
In all the universe we have no place.
Our wounds are hurting us; where is the balm?
Lord Jesus, by Thy Scars, we claim Thy grace.

If, when the doors are shut, Thou drawest near,
Only reveal those hands, that side of Thine;
We know to-day what wounds are, have no fear,
Show us Thy Scars, we know the countersign.

The other gods were strong; but Thou wast weak;
They rode, but Thou didst stumble to a throne;
But to our wounds only God's wounds can speak,
And not a god has wounds, but Thou alone.

Edward Shillito, "Jesus of the Scars"

THE THIRTEENTH STATION

Jesus is taken down from the cross

Scripture

After these things, Joseph of Arimathea, who was a disciple of Jesus, though a secret one because of his fear of the Jews, asked Pilate to let him take away the body of Jesus. Pilate gave him permission; so he came and removed his body. Nicodemus, who had at first come to Jesus by night, also came, bringing a mixture of myrrh and aloes, weighing about a hundred pounds. They took the body of Jesus and wrapped it with the spices in linen cloths, according to the burial custom of the Jews.

John 19:38-40

Reflection

In the absence of your disciples, dear Lord, your dead body is slowly and with great care lowered from the cross by two comparative strangers – Nicodemus and Joseph of Arimathea. Paradoxically both are elite officials of the Jerusalem government, not Galilean fishermen; both important decision-makers from the south, not northern country folk. Can geography ever divide us in the art of care?

Some time ago Nicodemus approached you under cover of darkness, caution on tiptoe, to talk to you alone. He did not even tell his wife that night where he was heading – secrecy was everything. At that time he was nervous about being seen in your company; now, on this pitiless Friday afternoon, he demonstrates his reverence for you.

The last time you met was when he whispered his concerns to you in that dark, sheltered grove in Gethsemane; now he meets you again in the light of day, in a public execution site, as the chief priests and the scribes glower their disapproval at him. He knows he will pay for this as he holds in his arms the truth he once heard: that God so loved the world that he risked his Son amidst its futile violence.

Joseph of Arimathea, a member of the Sanhedrin, the Jewish high council, is portrayed as your secret disciple, though that secrecy is now tossed aside by his unconcealed affection for you. Although he did not cast his vote against you in the council, he told no one of his abstention, just in case: the principal art in politics, after all, is to survive another day. Now Joseph's governing identity is not the grandee survivor but the devoted disciple.

From a safe distance Joseph has watched you pay the price, dear Lord, for loving the last and the least and the lost: you have shifted his heart from reserve to fervour. As an aristocrat, like to like, he had ready access to the Roman governor and has received permission to take your body down from the cross. Nothing secret, is there, about that? Pontius Pilate immediately instructed his intelligence service, "Monitor this new alliance with the Jesus movement."

Before burial, your body is now handed over to your waiting mother who has never been cautious or secretive about her love for you. As your crown of thorns falls off your head and onto the ground, your mother weeps such a rush of tears that it begins to wash the blood off your chest. As she held you in her arms as a child and washed you, she now holds you and washes you in death.

As the execution tourists press forward for a closer view, she ignores them. For her now, there are only two people in the world – everyone else is absent. She knows that when she buries you, her only son, she will also bury every hope she cherished, every dream she treasured about you in the shelter of her heart. She has kept so much in her heart that it has become a storeroom crammed with gathered sorrows. It is not just your body that will go into the tomb but her broken heart will accompany you there.

She strokes your right cheek, feeling the slackness of it and absorbing the coldness of it, flesh of her flesh. Your body seems strangely weightless to her, like it was when you were a child. She relives again that day you left Nazareth: she sees your retreating back, your urgency to get away, without looking back, never to return to a place that had no heart for who you yearned to be. Why did you go south and take on the important people, lacerating them in the public squares, telling the chief priests that the prostitutes would walk before them into the kingdom of God? So many questions.

She sees the others approach discreetly to take you from her and lay you to rest. Passover is approaching; the burial has to be completed. You leave life, dear Lord, as you came into it, in your mother's arms. She must let you go for the last time. She says, "Goodbye, son, I love you. Always have, always will, for evermore."

Humanity on the rocks

Nilüfer Demir was crossing a beach in Bodrum, Turkey, when she saw a small boy in a red T-shirt, blue trousers and black sneakers, lying face-down in the sand. The waves lapped at his lifeless face.

"There was nothing left to do for him. There was nothing left to bring him back to life," she told CNN. So Demir, a correspondent and photographer with a Turkish news agency, did the only thing she could: she raised her camera and began taking pictures. "There was nothing to do except take his photograph… and that is exactly what I did. I thought, this is the only way I can express the scream of his silent body."

Soon a Turkish police officer picks up and tenderly cradles the lifeless body of the Syrian-Kurdish child who was named by the Turkish state news agency as three-year-old Alan Kurdi. He drowned along with his five-year-old brother Galip and their mother as they aimed to reach the safety of the Greek island of Kos.

A total of five children and one woman were confirmed dead in the incident; seven others were rescued; two reached the shore in lifejackets.

Unlike the unnamed and countless litany of refugees who have drowned at sea, the dead body of little Alan was on the front of most of the world's newspapers. It is a heartbreaking picture of complete vulnerability, of innocence betrayed, of hope fragmented, of sanctuary unattained.

As Jesus was taken down tenderly from the cross, following his execution, and put into the arms of his beloved mother, the body of this little boy, following his death by drowning, is gently lifted from the shore by a stranger. All the real differences between the policeman and the boy are suddenly made irrelevant: the bond of humanity speaks to a fragmented world.

Prayer

Lord,
remember not only the men and the women
of good will but also all those of ill will.

Do not remember only the suffering
that they have inflicted on us,
but remember also the fruits we have brought,
thanks to this suffering:

our comradeship and our loyalty,
our humility and our courage,
the generosity and greatness of heart
which has grown out of all this.

And when those people come to judgement,
let all the fruits we have borne
be their forgiveness.

*Ravensbrück, situated north of Berlin, was the largest
concentration camp for women in the German Reich.
This prayer, scrawled on wrapping paper, was found
near the body of a dead child.*

THE FOURTEENTH STATION

Jesus is buried in the tomb

Scripture

So Joseph took the body and wrapped it in a clean linen cloth and laid it in his own new tomb, which he had hewn in the rock. He then rolled a great stone to the door of the tomb and went away. Mary Magdalene and the other Mary were there, sitting opposite the tomb.

The next day, that is, after the day of Preparation, the chief priests and the Pharisees gathered before Pilate and said, "Sir, we remember what that impostor said while he was still alive, 'After three days I will rise again.' Therefore command that the tomb be made secure until the third day; otherwise his disciples may go and steal him away, and tell the people, 'He has been raised from the dead,' and the last deception would be worse than the first." Pilate said to them, "You have a guard of soldiers; go, make it as secure as you can." So they went with the guard and made the tomb secure by sealing the stone.

Matthew 27:59-66

Reflection

Your new wholehearted disciple, Joseph of Arimathea, kindly wraps your body in swaddling cloth, using a thin gauzelike fabric that he hopes will serve to keep your limbs together. He then carefully places your body in his new tomb, on a ledge cut out from the rock – the very place he had prepared for himself. As it is a new tomb there are no other bodies lying there, but deeper into the cave there is a small chamber which houses a waiting ossuary, a box for bones; this is traditional practice, I believe, so that when decomposition is complete the bones will be collected and placed in the box, freeing the ledge for the next body.

Standing back, Joseph, somewhat breathless, reviews his arrangement of your body and then returns to reposition your hands with care. They are obediently rearranged as you had them when the soldiers stripped you of your clothes. After a final inspection Joseph feels that he has laid you out well. Of course he has no idea what a temporary tenant you will be.

Outside, the women – experts in the art of standing by – linger opposite the tomb. They watch Joseph emerge into the fading light, marking how he struggles to roll the stone against the entrance, heaving and panting all the while. When she hears the emphatic thud of stone on stone, Mary of Magdala feels it sounds like the last heartbeat of the earth itself. Then, ever practical, she moves to wondering how they will manage to move that stone when they return to anoint the body. Will any of the men, she wonders, be around to help them?

The next day the religious authorities are still nervous about you, dear Lord, even when you lie dead: they worry your disciples might steal your body and then claim that you are risen from the dead. To keep them off his back, Pilate gives them permission to set a guard: I believe it was normal for a Roman guard to consist of four soldiers, with one on watch while the others rested or slept, to be awakened readily at any alarm. It is interesting that Pilate does not share with them the information his intelligence service has provided: that all your disciples, dear Lord, have abandoned you and returned north to Galilee, which is outside his domain. Nobody will be around, he knows, to steal your body.

Delighted that the governor has agreed with their caution, the chief priests and the Pharisees hurry out and seal the stone into the entrance of the tomb. That way no one and nothing can gain entrance to the tomb: you, dear Lord, are now beyond the reach of any human contact. They leave you alone eternally to leave them in peace.

If death had spoken the final word about you, dear Lord, it would only have been a matter of time before everything about you would have been reduced to a curiosity, a forgettable footnote in the crowded history of lost causes. The memory of you and all you had done would have faded within a couple of generations. But our Father had the last word – as indeed the first.

This tomb is a special sanctuary because it will witness what no other human being will witness – God's refusal to leave you, his beloved Son, to rest in peace. No RIP will ever be written over your borrowed tomb.

In this darkest of places there will soon be the brightest light in the world. This tomb, dear Lord, will be a voiceless witness to God's liberating and lasting love for you, his respect for all your struggles and his eternal gratitude to you. Resurrection will be our Father's response to the cross, his defiant answer to the powers that hoped violence could keep you in hold. In raising you from the dead God will raise every value you stood for, every story you ever told, every choice you ever made and every purpose you ever hallowed. All that you did and said will be given new life and new significance.

Dear Lord, this tomb can never be your permanent address: you will have no alternative but to rise to the occasion.

Remembering the dead

Emmanuel Bizimana, who was born two years before the 1994 genocide in Rwanda, is consoled by a friend while attending a public ceremony to mark the twentieth anniversary of the Rwandan genocide. This commemoration took place at the main stadium in Kigali in April 2014. Although he was not part of the disaster, his face expresses hurt and bewilderment at the unimaginable tragedy. Who knows what personal loss he is recalling? Official estimates of the dead range between eight hundred thousand and one million Rwandans who perished in three months of machete and gunfire attacks, mostly by extremist Hutus on the country's minority Tutsi population.

Ever since the massacre, the international community has been forced to concede it stood by and did nothing. The UN chief told a news conference he hopes to reaffirm the international community's commitment to the idea of "never again".

Death is not just a fate that we meet at the end of life – we see death all around us in the midst of life: the economic death of the people who fade away from malnutrition; the political death of all those who are oppressed; the raging death that strikes through torture and explosives and suicide bombers.

To accept this litany of death as inevitable is to render worthless the power of the Gospel. A resurrection faith faces the cross and protests against the finality of that violence. It educates us to see as God sees; to act as so many of God's chosen do act today when with enormous courage they refuse to genuflect to the powers of darkness. If the resurrection means anything in life it is a refusal to accept that anyone should be left for dead.

In the words of the American poet Adrienne Rich:

> My heart is moved by all I cannot save:
> so much has been destroyed.
> I have to cast my lot with those
> who age after age, perversely,
> with no extraordinary power,
> reconstitute the world.[7]

Prayer

"Arise, my love, my fair one,
and come away;
for now the winter is past,
the rain is over and gone.
The flowers appear on the earth;
the time of singing has come,
and the voice of the turtle-dove
is heard in our land.
The fig tree puts forth its figs,
and the vines are in blossom;
they give forth fragrance.
Arise, my love, my fair one,
and come away."

O you who dwell in the gardens,
my companions are listening for your voice;
let me hear it.

Song of Solomon 2:10-13; 8:13

References

1. Seamus Heaney, "Weighing In", in *The Spirit Level* (London: Faber and Faber, 1996), 17.

2. Patrick Kavanagh, "Lough Derg", in *Collected Poems,* ed. Antoinette Quinn (London: Penguin Books, 2005), 90.

3. W.H. Auden, "Musée des Beaux Arts", in *Collected Poems*, ed. Edward Mendelson (New York: Random House, 1976), 146-147.

4. Dorothee Sölle, *Suffering* (Philadelphia: Fortress Press, 1975), 32.

5. Primo Levi, *The Drowned and the Saved* (London: Abacus, 1988), 90.

6. Alan Seeger, "I Have a Rendezvous with Death", in *Rendezvous with Death*: *American Poems of the Great War,* ed. Mark W. Van Wienen (Urbana: University of Illinois Press, 2002), 142.

7. Adrienne Rich, "Natural Resources", in *The Dream of a Common Language: Poems 1974–1977* (New York: W.W. Norton, 1993), 60.

Picture acknowledgements: Front cover and throughout, Stations of the Cross: Zvonimir Atletic/Shutterstock.com; Front cover and p106: Nilufer Demir/Getty; p10: Bizutage (own work) [CC BY-SA 3.0 (http://creativecommons.org/licenses/by-sa/3.0)], via Wikimedia Commons; p18: Gustava Guttierez; p26: European Pressphoto Agency; p 34: Javier Paredes (own work) [CC BY-SA 3.0 (http://creativecommons.org/licenses/by-sa/3.0)], via Wikimedia Commons; p42: Achilleas Zavallis/Getty; p 50: Jean-Claude Francolon/Getty; p58: Horacio Arevalo (IMG_0257.jpg) [CC BY-SA 3.0 (http://creativecommons.org/licenses/by-sa/3.0)], via Wikimedia Commons; p 66: Bulent Kilic/Getty; p74: Jeff Christiensen/Reuters Pictures; p82: Everett Historical/Shutterstock.com; p 90: VanderWolf Images/Shutterstock.com; p98: Francesco Tuccio; p114: Ben Curtis/Press Association.

Every effort has been made to trace copyright holders and to obtain their permission for the use of copyright material. The publisher apologises for any errors or omissions and would be grateful for notification of any corrections that should be incorporated in future reprints or editions of this book.